G.C

HIGH BLOOD PRESSURE
3rd Edition

THE EIGHT LAWS OF HEALTH
AND THEIR THERAPEUTIC VALUE
IN THE RECOVERY FROM
HIGH BLOOD PRESSURE

A Publication of:

M.E.E.T. Ministry
Missionary Education and Evangelistic Training
480 Neely Lane
Huntingdon, TN 38344
Phone (731) 986-3518
Fax (731) 986-0582
E-mail: godsplan@meetministry.org
Web Site: www.meetministry.org

Contributions

GOD'S PLAN

God

Manuscript
Shelem Flemons
Thomas Jackson: Introduction
Jean Boatright: Power To Change

Research Contributions
Thomas Jackson
Duane R. Smith
Shelem Flemons
Ann Mayfield

Art and Layout
Joan Frank
Joya Jones
Layout and Design
Dea Davis
Cover Design

Review and Editing
Janice Maywether

Health and Happiness Library Series

"Sickness abounds for want of sound, practical life-style education. I have grown to appreciate your emphasis on the simple life-style principles given in the Bible which contain the therapeutic properties handcrafted by the Creator. GOD'S PLAN is indeed the best plan. Keep up the good work." R. Blackburn, M.D., Texas

"The health and happiness library series has really helped me understand more about God's plan for health. I have been able to help many people in my country using the simple remedies found in nature. I look forward to the other books in this series."
F. Sue, Registered Nurse, Taiwan

"I have appreciated the simple biblical approach to health that M.E.E.T. ministry promotes through its publications. The eight laws of health have been a spiritual, mental and physical blessing to my congregation."

Important!

The information presented in this book is based on God's original life-style plan as it is presented in the Holy Bible. This information is provided for educational purposes only and is not intended as treatment for an individual's health concerns or ailments.

Furthermore, the information in this book is not intended as either medical advice, diagnosis, or prescription. The publisher assumes no responsibility for any adverse conditions or consequences that may result from the use or misuse of the information presented in this book.

Table of Contents

Introduction

There is an astonishing promise in the Bible that most Americans have yet to benefit from. It is found in the book of Exodus, chapter 15, verse 26; and it reads as follows: *"If thou wilt diligently hearken to the voice of the Lord thy God, and wilt do that which is right in His sight, and wilt give ear to His commandments and keep all His statutes,* **I will put none of these diseases upon thee which I have brought upon the Egyptians, for I am the Lord that healeth thee."** *Exodus 15:26.*

What is the significance of this promise? What were the diseases of the Egyptians from which God promised deliverance? As paleopathologists (scientists who study ancient diseases) have uncovered the mummified bodies of the Egyptians which were contemporary with the Biblical era,

 remarkable findings have been disclosed. Incredibly, the Egyptians also suffered from the same diseases that are presently plaguing millions of Americans every year. They found arthritis, cancer, heart disease, diabetes, and **all the symptoms commonly associated with high blood pressure**.

Seeing then that our Father in heaven promised that *"NONE OF THESE DISEASES"* would plague us if we were obedient, 40 million Americans who presently suffer from high blood pressure would be delivered from this silent killer. This would drastically improve the lives and usefulness of one out of every six Americans who are presently the unfortunate victims of hypertension (the medical term for high blood pressure).

God's promise of physical, mental and spiritual health is little realized and the conditions for receiving the promise are given little value in our life-style priority lists. As a result, the health of the American people is not improving; it is getting worse. Despite the advances in medical science, American workers lead the world in degenerative diseases. Because of disease, it is estimated that over $385 million a day is lost from work; $200 million a day is lost in school absences, and the total cost of health care exceeds $420 billion - that's *__420 billion dollars__*, enough to cut in half the projected national deficit in 1995.

What do the traditional treatments for high blood pressure have to offer the American people? The first approach in treating hypertension with conventional methods is to prescribe mild drugs first. These drugs can generally be placed in three categories. The first category consists of drugs which have a diuretic effect on the body. A diuretic drug is one that causes increased urination in an effort to expel excess fluids which tend to accumulate in the body of a person with high blood pressure. The second category of drugs consists of those medications which cause the heart to pump less blood. This can lower the pressure because there is less blood flowing through the arteries and veins. The third category of drugs include prescriptions which lower the resistance of the vessels to the blood which flows from the heart.

The mild drugs prescribed at first have relatively few side effects in comparison with the more potent drugs which hypertensive patients usually take. The problem with all drugs whether mild or more intense is that they do not address the cause of the problem they are seeking to cure. The Bible declares that every disease has a cause. (See Proverbs 26:3). It was God's plan that the cause of every disease or symptom be reversed rather than just treating the symptoms with drugs. The mild drugs with fewer side effects almost always lead to the more potent drugs with serious side effects which often cause more problems than the elevated blood pressure itself.

The major problem with high blood pressure is that it is a serious risk factor for cardiovascular diseases such as heart attack and stroke which are the top killers in the United States.

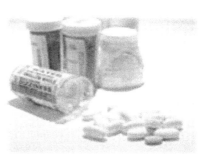

The purpose of **GOD'S PLAN - HEALTH AND HAPPINESS LIBRARY SERIES** is to reveal the wonderful therapeutic value of the eight natural remedies that our Creator merged together into a **SIMPLE** and **ABSOLUTELY FREE** life-style package that would almost completely deliver us from the massive burden of disease which plagues the world. These eight laws which originated in the Garden of Eden will *"take the pressure off"* and will prove to be a remedy for every other ailment. Obedience to these laws is our only hope of making God's promise of health and happiness a genuine reality.

The Fence or the Ambulance

Twas a dangerous cliff as they freely confessed,
Though to walk near its crest was so pleasant;
But over its terrible edge there had slipped
A duke and many a peasant;
So the people said something would have to be done,
But their projects did not at all tally:
Some said, "Put a fence round the edge of the cliff";
Some, "An ambulance down in the valley."

But the cry for the ambulance carried the day,
For it spread to the neighboring city;
A fence may be useful or not, it is true,
But each heart became brimful of pity
For those who had slipped o'er that dangerous cliff,
And the dwellers in highway and alley
Gave pounds or gave pence, not to put up a fence,
But an ambulance down in the valley.

"For the cliff is all right if you're careful," they said;
"And if folks even slip or are dropping,
It isn't the slipping that hurts them so much
As the shock down below - when they're stopping."
So day after day when these mishaps occurred,
Quick forth would the rescuers sally
To pick up the victims who fell off the cliff
With their ambulance down in the valley.

Then an old man remarked: "It's a marvel to me
That people give far more attention
To repairing results than to stopping the cause,
When they'd much better aim at prevention.
Let us stop at its source all this mischief," cried he,
"Come neighbors and friends, let us rally;

If the cliff we will fence, we might almost dispense
With the ambulance down in the valley."

"Oh, he's a fanatic," the others rejoined;
"Dispense with the ambulance? Never!
He'd dispense with all charities, too, if he could;
No, no! We'll support them forever.
Aren't we picking up folks just as fast as they fall?
And shall this man dictate to us? Shall he?
Why should people of sense stop to put up a fence,
While their ambulance works in the valley?"

Thus this story so old has beautifully told
How our people with best of intentions,
Have wasted their years and lavished their tears
On treatment, with naught for prevention.

But a sensible few who are practical too,
Will not bear with such nonsense much longer;
They believe that prevention is better than cure
And their party will soon be the stronger.
Encourage them, then, with your purse, voice, and pen,
And (while other philanthropists dally)
They will scorn all pretense, and put up a stout fence
On the cliff that hangs over the valley.

-Joseph Malines

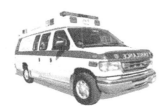

Enjoy your reading. We at M.E.E.T. Publishing are sure that you will find in the eight laws of health, God's Plan for the preservation and restoration of health!

Understanding the Nature of High Blood Pressure

"Give me understanding, and I shall keep thy Law."
Psalm 119:34.

The human body is made up of many trillions of cells. It is these cells which do all the work within the body to keep us healthy and insure that all bodily processes are functioning properly. In order for cells of the body to do their appointed work, they must receive a constant supply of oxygen and nutrients, as well as have an avenue to release their wastes. This avenue is called the blood. Every cell needs a constant supply of this blood in order to survive. To insure that enough blood reaches every cell that needs it, God has designed within the human being a constant force called blood pressure to propel this life giving fluid through arteries, veins, and capillaries. Blood pressure is the force that moves blood to the various points in the body where the nutrients, oxygen and wastes need to be dropped off. If the pressure becomes too low, this can be very dangerous for the cells will not receive enough blood. Dangerously low blood pressure is very rare and usually accompanies some type of trauma with a significant amount of blood loss.

The problem with most people is that the pressure of the blood flowing through the arteries becomes too high. This condition is probably the most significant risk factor in heart attacks and strokes along with other physical problems.

Blood pressure is measured with a blood pressure cuff called a sphygmomanometer and a stethoscope. Blood pressure is expressed with two numbers. The first number is called the systolic pressure and should be 120 (plus or minus 20). This represents the pressure of blood when the heart is beating. The second number is called the diastolic pressure and this number represents the pressure between heart beats or the resting pressure. Normal diastolic 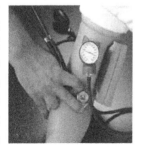 should be 80 (plus or minus 10). Therefore a normal blood pressure would be expressed as 120 over 80 or any numbers within the acceptable ranges previously listed.

To understand the nature of high blood pressure, it is helpful to imagine a factory with many workers. The "life blood" of this factory consists of an essential fluid which all the factory workers need and have access to twenty-four hours a day in order to perform their work. This essential fluid reaches each work site within the factory through an enormous pipeline which is dispersed throughout the factory with many drop-off and pick-up points along the way. The central focus of this factory is a huge electric pump so powerful that it is able to successfully pump this fluid through the many, many miles of pipeline so that every worker has the essentials he needs. With proper maintenance, this pump carries a 120 year warranty by the manufacturer. It is strong and durable and should not wear out prematurely.

To protect the life of the pump, there are gauges along the pipeline which measure the amount of pressure against inner walls of the pipes. If the pressure drops too low the maintenance crew is notified and they immediately suspect a leak in the pipeline which is allowing vital fluids to escape. Severely low pressure however is very rare at this factory and constitutes emergency measures because some or all of the workers will not be able to receive enough of the vital fluid in order to do their specific jobs. If a severely low pressure problem is not corrected immediately, it will cause the pump to stop working, the workers will not have what they need to perform, and the factory will go out of business.

Fortunately, severely low pressure problems are very rare and almost unheard of. There is, unfortunately a more widespread and equally dangerous problem with which the maintenance crew has to contend. This problem occurs when the pressure within the pipes becomes too high. This makes the pump work too hard and is a sign that this pump, along with the entire factory of workers is in serious trouble. The problem is that a factory with a high pressure problem can indeed still function for several years without realizing that its pump is prematurely aging and the productivity of its workers cut in half. Over the years, the nickname, *"Silent Killer"* was given to the high pressure emergency because some inexperienced maintenance crews allowed it to go on unattended, thinking that it would not affect the overall activity of the factory. The *Silent Killer* cuts short the life of the pump, and when it suddenly gives up the ghost it is often too late to fix it.

This vital pump, if you haven't already guessed, is the heart. The miles and miles of pipeline represent the arteries, veins and capillaries; and the essential fluid which is provided for the workers is the blood.

What happens in the body when the blood pressure rises? The changes that occur in the body when the blood pressure is elevated can be grouped into seven categories. If you the reader can understand these seven simple occurrences, you will understand better than some professionals the nature of high blood pressure, and how to lower it. Try to memorize them. After reading this chapter, you will be well prepared to understand the next chapter which discusses the causes of high blood pressure.

By the way, the term "hypertension" is the same as "high blood pressure", so from here on the two terms will be used interchangeably.

When the pressure is elevated, one or more of these characteristics below are always present.

High Blood Pressure Occurs When:

1. **THE HEART PUMPS FASTER** **This causes more blood to be pumped through the arteries. The rush of blood raises the pressure.**

2. **THE BLOOD VESSELS CONSTRICT** **As these vessels become smaller the blood pressure rises because it takes more pressure to move the blood through a smaller place.**

3. **THERE IS AN INCREASE OF BLOOD VOLUME** **This simply means that there is more blood than necessary. This occurs when the body retains water. This water mixes with the blood and causes more fluid to pass through the vessels because the heart must now pump the excess water that has been added to the blood.**

4. **THERE IS A PARTIAL BLOCKAGE OF ONE OR MORE OF THE BLOOD VESSELS** **A clogged artery raises pressure because the blood has to squeeze through the partial blockage.**

5. **THERE ARE TOXINS IN THE BLOOD WHICH CREATE A TRAFFIC JAM WITHIN THE BLOOD VESSELS** When toxins aren't eliminated from various organs of the body, they are reabsorbed into the bloodstream creating a "Rush Hour Traffic" effect. (TOO MANY VEHICLES ON THE HIGHWAY)

6. **THE KIDNEYS AND/OR LIVER ARE NOT FUNCTIONING PROPERLY** All of the blood in circulation must flow through these organs. When they are not functioning properly, they create a slow down in traffic similar to that seen on the highway near construction sites or the scene of an accident.

7. **THE INDIVIDUAL WITH HYPERTENSION IS OBESE** The extra fat in the body add miles and miles of blood vessels through which the heart must pump blood. The load on the heart is greater because of the larger and longer blood vessels. It takes more pressure to push the blood through the longer distances.

What Causes High Blood Pressure?

"The cause which I knew not, I searched out."
Job 29:16.

As the previous chapter suggested, there are seven problems that occur in the body which lead to high blood pressure. This chapter will discuss the causes of these seven problems one by one so that you will have a clear understanding of the problem of high blood pressure and its causes. The remainder of this book will discuss the prevention and cure of this almost universal ailment.

Category #1

Things that make the heart pump faster.

As the heart beats faster it pumps more blood

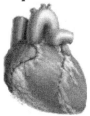

This Raises the blood pressure

This problem is caused by **stress**. When we are under stress, the body is preparing for the "fight or flight response". Imagine that you were awakened from your sleep by your son or daughter yelling "Fire!" What would happen to your heart? It would receive the following message from your brain, "Heart, beat faster so you can push more blood to the legs and arms of the person you're beating for. More blood is needed immediately because he is encountering an emergency!" As the heart pumps more blood, it causes the blood pressure to rise by providing more blood to be pumped through the vessels.

This problem is also caused by consuming **drugs such as nicotine from tobacco, caffeine from many of the popular soft drinks, and theobromine from chocolate.** These "drugs" make your body think that the house is on fire. The heart responds the same way.

Last but not least, **consuming refined white sugar** in desserts, candies, and soft drinks produces a similar effect because of the way that the body responds to the sugar. Sugar is not a food, it's a drug!

Category #2

Things that make the blood vessels constrict

To constrict means to become smaller. Blood vessels are flexible and elastic, therefore they have the unique ability of responding to certain conditions in the body by constricting or dilating (becoming larger).

Stress is again the first point we will discuss in our list of blood vessel constricting causes. When the body senses that an emergency is present and prepares itself by increasing the heart rate, the blood passing through the extremities increases in speed. This presents a problem to the cells in the legs and arms that need nutrients, water and oxygen from the blood. The heart is now pumping the blood so fast that the cells are not able to get any nutrients out of the blood. To compensate for this, the body responds by constricting the blood vessels in an effort to slow the blood down. This enables the cells in the legs and arms to get the nutrients from the blood and to expel their wastes into the blood to be taken to other parts of the body for elimination.

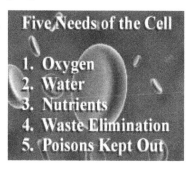

Five Needs of the Cell
1. Oxygen
2. Water
3. Nutrients
4. Waste Elimination
5. Poisons Kept Out

The problem is that with this stress response, the blood pressure rises. This is because the blood vessels have narrowed causing the blood now to be forced through constricted channels. It takes more pressure to push the blood through the narrower vessels than before the stress response.

Another causative factor in restricted blood vessels is **insufficiently clothing the extremities.** As the legs and arms are brought into contact with colder temperatures than that of the trunk area of the body, the blood vessels constrict in an effort to hold in the heat. This raises blood pressure.

Another cause that has been mentioned in category #1 is that of **drugs such as nicotine, caffeine, theobromine, and sugar.** These substances cause the adrenals to secrete a hormone called adrenaline which constricts the blood vessels.

Category #3

There is an increase of blood volume

An increase of blood volume simply means that the amount of blood that the heart must pump has now increased. The primary cause of an increase of blood volume is the consumption of too much **sodium.** For most Americans on the "Standard American Diet" (S.A.D. see page 46), this excess sodium is introduced into the body through table salt. Most Americans buy foods that are already high in sodium such as processed canned or packaged foods. We then add a liberal amount of salt to these foods when cooking them. Instead of quitting while we're ahead, we then add more salt to these foods once they are on our plates.

Sodium causes the body to retain water. Much of this excess water that the body is now retaining is absorbed into the bloodstream and increases the total blood volume. The heart then has the added burden of pumping all the excess water that has been added to the blood. **THE BLOOD VESSELS LITERALLY BECOME OBESE AND THE PRESSURE AGAINST THE WALLS OF THE ARTERIES IN-CREASES.**

This condition is also an indication of a **lack of potassium.** This is because sodium outside of the cells works with potassium inside the cells to form a pump which allows wastes to leave the cells and nutrients to enter into the cells.

Another causative factor in the increase of blood volume is the **overconsumption of protein foods**. When a person consumes more protein than the body can handle, the body treats this protein as it would a poison and tries to get rid of it. Because every eliminative process within the body requires water, more fluid is retained in an effort to eliminate the toxins that have developed as a result of consuming too much protein.

Category #4

There is a partial blockage of one or more blood vessels

The primary cause of a blockage within the arteries is the condition called atherosclerosis. This condition is characterized by a buildup of fats, calcium deposits, and fibrin within the arteries. These plaques form blood clots and decrease the diameter through which blood must flow. They literally clog the arteries. If a main artery leading to the heart becomes completely blocked with these cholesterol plaques, a person will have a heart attack. If an artery leading to the brain becomes blocked, the result is a stroke.

The blood clot actually begins with some damage in the artery wall. Blood fats and calcium deposits tend to collect at the site in an effort to heal the damaged area. The initial damage to the artery wall is often caused by harmful substances called free radicals. Free radicals have the ability to enter the cells and alter the DNA. This can cause the size of the damaged area within the artery to increase because the cells in the artery wall may multiply rapidly. This weblike

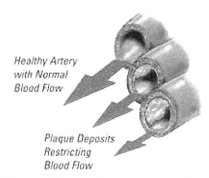

Healthy Artery
with Normal
Blood Flow

Plaque Deposits
Restricting
Blood Flow

Clogged arteries restrict the flow of blood and raises the blood pressure

plaque catches some of the blood fats that are flowing in the blood stream and the clot becomes larger and larger.

These blood clots affect blood pressure because now blood must be forced through areas in the arteries in which the diameter has decreased.

It takes more pressure to push the blood through a smaller space. A good analogy is that traffic always slows down at the scene of an accident.

Category #5

Excess toxins within the body

The Bible declares that "The life of the flesh is in the blood." *Lev. 17:11*. The blood carries the wastes from cell metabolism or from the poisons that we ingest to organs where they can be eliminated. When these poisons become too numerous because of poor elimination through the colon, lungs, or other organs, the wastes build up in the blood stream and contribute to high blood pressure. **A major contributing factor in high blood pressure is constipation.**

Category #6

The kidneys and liver are not functioning properly

The kidneys are responsible for eliminating liquid wastes from the body. They also have the responsibility of eliminating sodium. When they are not functioning properly there is a back up of liquid wastes in the body and a slow down of blood flow in the renal artery leading to each kidney. Poor dietary habits, a lack of pure water, smoking, and the consumption of coffee or tea are among the causes of kidney damage.

The blood which flows through the stomach, intestines, spleen, and pancreas passes through the liver via the portal vein before returning to the heart. The liver performs many functions including the metabolism of fats, carbohydrates, and protein. When its function is impaired either through overconsumption of protein, fats, or refined carbohydrates, along with drugs such as caffeine, nicotine and alcohol, there is a back up of blood flow into the portal vein. This condition is called portal hypertension and this high blood pressure in the portal vein is reflected in the entire body.

Category #7

<u>The individual with hypertension is obese</u>

The more obesity that a person has, the more blood vessels are needed to supply the extra fat cells with needed blood. A few extra pounds can literally add miles and miles of blood vessels through which the heart must now pump blood. This causes the pressure to rise in an effort to pump blood through the distant vessels. The major causes are directly related to our eating and drinking habits, along with our amount of physical exercise. Most Americans eat the wrong food in the wrong way, at the wrong time. We also lack daily physical exercise. Following the principles in this book will help a person lose weight naturally and keep it off!

"Let us hear the conclusion of the whole matter!"
Ecclesiastes 12:13.

The causes of high blood pressure can be grouped into seven categories.

1. <u>**The causes of increased heart rate are:**</u> stress, drugs such as nicotine, caffeine and theobromine, and the body's response to overconsuming refined white sugar.

2. <u>**The causes of blood vessels constricting are:**</u> stress, insufficiently clothing the extremities, and certain drugs such as nicotine, caffeine and sugar.

3. <u>**The causes of increased blood volume include:**</u> excess sodium in the body, a lack of potassium, and overconsumption of protein.

4. <u>**The cause of blocked arteries is:**</u> the build up of fats, calcium deposits and fibrin into plaque formations within the arteries. This condition is called atherosclerosis.

5. <u>**The cause of increased toxins in the blood is:**</u> poor elimination from the colon, lungs and other organs. Violating any of the eight laws of health make a person more susceptible to high blood pressure.

6. <u>**The causes of impaired kidneys include:**</u> poor dietary habits, lack of pure water, smoking, and caffeine consumption

<u>**The causes of impaired liver function include:**</u> an overconsumption of protein, fats, and refined carbohydrates, consuming caffeine and alcohol and tobacco.

7. <u>**The causes of obesity are:**</u> related to our habits of eating and exercise.

Godly Trust

"Trust in the Lord with all thine heart, and lean not unto thine own understanding... It shall be health to thy navel and marrow to thy bones." Proverbs 3:5-8.

The Bible declares that, *"A merry heart doeth good like a medicine, but a broken spirit drieth the bones." Proverbs 17:22.* When we are happy and cheerful, a hormone called endorphin is produced in our bodies. This hormone is called our "happy hormone" and comes as a result of a trusting relationship with our Saviour Jesus Christ. "Whoso *trusteth in the Lord, happy is he." Proverbs 16:20.*

Godly Trust is the foremost antidote for stress. It is absolutely essential that those who have high blood pressure eliminate the stress producing effects of worry, anxiety and fear because these emotions cause a chain reaction within the body which raises the blood pressure. Under stress, the adrenal glands send out hormones which cause the heart to beat faster, the blood vessels to constrict, and the blood fats to increase. This is because the body is preparing for an emergency and is sending more blood to the extremities. When stress is prolonged, the adrenal glands tend to become exhausted and other essential functions such as increasing the output of hydrochloric acid and pepsin in the stomach cannot be done adequately by these stressed out glands. These digestive juices are necessary for the proper digestion of protein. When protein is not properly digested, foreign protein enters the bloodstream through the small intestines and these foreign proteins place a burden on the liver which must assist in detoxifying these poisons.

Keep in mind that one of the "Seven Pressure Points" discussed earlier is that hypertension is also caused by an overburdened liver. When its function is impaired, there is a traffic jam in the portal vein leading to the liver which increases the overall blood pressure.

Stress also lowers the body's levels of potassium. This condition causes the body to retain fluids which raise blood pressure.

The first step in applying this trust to our lives is accepting Jesus Christ into our lives as our personal Saviour. This involves surrendering our lives to Jesus Christ. Christ said, *"Ye must be born again." John 3:7.*

We must repent of our sins, asking God to forgive us and cleanse us from all unrighteousness. (See 1 John 1:9). We must ask God to forgive us for disobeying His natural laws which have brought on disease. He will forgive us! He will cleanse us, and give us power to live a new life. *"Walk in the Spirit, and ye shall not fulfil the lust of the flesh." Galatians 5:16.*

God has placed many promises in the Bible for us. We are to read His promises, believe them, and act upon them. As Christians, we understand that our first duty is to love and obey God. He said, *"For this is the love of God, that we keep His commandments: and His commandments are not grievous." 1 John 5:3.* When we are assailed by temp-

tations and obstacles, we should quote the scripture just as Jesus did. *"It is written"* was the Saviour's weapon against the devil, and David wrote, *"Thy word have I hid in mine heart that I might not sin against thee." Psalm 119:11.* As we study the word of God, fear and discouragement will give way to hope and courage, and this change in our thoughts will actually add to our healing process. The Bible says, "A good report maketh the bones fat." Proverbs 15:30. The Bible is a book of good reports.

Another essential application of Godly Trust is prayer. When we pray, we should always end our prayer as Jesus did when He said, *"Thy will be done." Matthew 6:10.* In so doing, we are submitting our lives into the hands of God, knowing that He knows what is best for us. Prayer is essential for healing. We need to trust our case to the Great Physician realizing that no matter what happens to us here, we can spend eternity with Him if we are faithful.

Trust in God increases as we tell others what God has done for us. **We should always be ready to tell others how God is working in our lives. Witnessing to others will bring us even closer to God.**

Finally, it is important that we worship with our families morning and evening. This should be in addition to our personal devotions in the morning.

"Let us hear the conclusion of the whole matter!" Ecclesiastes 12:13.

Without Godly Trust, there will be stress. Stress will cause the adrenals to secrete hormones which will raise the blood pressure by increasing the heart rate and constricting the blood vessels. Prolonged stress will lessen the ability of the adrenals to secrete hormones, which will increase the production of hydrochloric acid and pepsin in the stomach. These digestive juices aid the stomach in its work of digesting protein. If protein is not digested properly in the stomach, the liver will be burdened with an excess of undigested proteins. A burdened liver is a primary cause of hypertension because it causes a traffic jam in the portal vein leading to the liver.

Godly Trust is the same as faith as it is taught in the scriptures. The scriptures tell us that, *"God hath dealt to every man the measure of faith." Romans 12:3.* This means that God has given the ability to exercise **Godly Trust** to every human being. What we do with this ability to trust is up to us.

"Without faith (Godly Trust) it is impossible to please Him." Hebrews 1:6.

Open Air

"And God said, Let there be a firmament in the midst of the waters; and let it divide the waters from the waters."
Genesis 1:6.

Fresh air, composed of 78% Nitrogen, 21% oxygen and 1% of other gases is crucial to our existence. The hundreds of trillions of cells of the human body are known as "aerobic" cells. This means that without adequate oxygen they begin to die. As a matter of fact, if we were deprived of oxygen, we would only have a few minutes to live.

One of the "Seven Pressure Points" previously listed is that of clogged arteries due to cholesterol and calcium plaques which build up in the blood vessel walls. This condition is known as atherosclerosis. These plaques begin with small sores that form in the walls of the arteries. The plaque formation is partially the body's effort to bandage the wounded artery. These wounds are formed more readily when the cells are lacking oxygen. This is because the cells which form the artery wall cannot properly remove their wastes when there is a lack of oxygen in the bloodstream.

Fresh air inspires every cell of the body and purifies the blood, causing the body to rapidly eliminate toxic wastes. As we inhale, oxygen seeps through the alveoli, tiny air sacs in the lungs, and vitalizes the bloodstream. As we exhale, carbon dioxide which neutralizes healthy cells, is eliminated.

Oxygen accelerates healing. It is the key ingredient which the body uses to manufacture **energy.** Oxygen combines with glucose, creating the chemical ATP which we recognize as energy. Very rarely is a person deficient in glucose, but it is often the case that there is a lack of oxygen. When energy levels are low, all of the functions of the body are inhibited, because they all require energy to do their jobs satisfactorily. When a person has atherosclerosis, his need for oxygen is even greater because the path of blood flow is partially blocked.

The body also uses oxygen as a detoxifying agent. Every metabolic function of the body leaves wastes behind. These wastes in the presence of oxygen can be easily expelled from the system.

Open Air also carries electrical charges. We refer to these charges as negative and positive ions. The more negative ions in the air, the healthier it is. This is because negative ions destroy substances called free radicals. These groups of compounds or atoms are the primary substances which cause the irritation in the walls of arteries which leads to atherosclerosis. Free radicals tend to al-

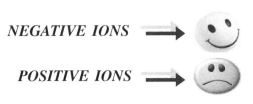

NEGATIVE IONS ⟹

POSITIVE IONS ⟹

ter the proper function of cells and therefore lead to cancer and atherosclerosis (plaque build up in the arteries). The negative ions in open air destroy these harmful free radicals. On the other hand free radicals flourish in an atmosphere where positive ions are plentiful.

Negative ions also act as an overall tonic for the body, causing one to feel refreshed and exhilarated. **Open Air** is absolutely essential in keeping the internal environment pure, and provides the cells with oxygen, their most essential need, and negative ions, which destroy free radicals.

As fresh air enters our homes it quickly adheres to walls and furnishings losing its life giving charge. Therefore, it is **Open Air** that is most therapeutic.

We must go out into the Open Air and breathe deeply in order to equalize the circulation of blood and provide every cell with its proper share of oxygen. **When we breathe properly The stomach should go out as we inhale and then return to its former position as we exhale**. Observing a newborn, it will be noticed that God has instilled in them proper breathing techniques. These habits change as the child grows older and begins to wear tight clothing around the waist which restricts the breathing process. **We should wear loose fitting clothing especially around the waist, and the weight of our clothing should be suspended from the shoulders instead of the waist. Wearing suspenders is much healthier than wearing belts.**

Most people do not breathe deeply enough and as a result, the chest goes out when they inhale and relaxes when they exhale. When the breathing is shallow, only the upper part of the lungs are being used, allowing wastes to build up in the lower part of the lungs.

Deep breathing takes practice and the following exercise should be done three times a day.

Inhale as deeply as possible and hold to a count of twenty. Exhale slowly. Wait ten seconds before inhaling again. In the open air, repeat this exercise twenty times in the morning, at noon and in the evening.

We cannot be in the open air all the time, **but we should always keep some windows cracked in our homes and work places even in winter** so that a constant supply of fresh air is received by the body. While sleeping, it is still important to have fresh air. We should not sleep under a draft, but we can still open at least two windows in the house, at least one to two inches high to receive some cross ventilation. **Open Air** is an indispensable ingredient in recovery from high blood pressure.

"Let us hear the conclusion of the whole matter!"
Ecclesiastes 12:13.

Open Air supplies the body with oxygen and negative ions. Oxygen accelerates healing, detoxifies the body, and provides energy for repair and rebuilding. Negative ions help to destroy free radicals which lead to atherosclerosis.

Daily Exercise

"I must walk today, and tomorrow, and the day following."
Luke 13:33.

We have already discussed the importance of oxygen in keeping blood vessel cells in good shape. As we **Exercise** in the open air, the muscles call for much more oxygen in order to produce energy. To supply this expedient need, the rate of breathing increases and the blood vessels expand. The heart rate also increases in order to pump the fresh oxygen to the muscle cells. The major benefit derived from **Exercise** is that while the muscle cells are receiving a fresh dose of oxygen, all the other cells in the body are oxygenated as a fringe benefit. As more cells receive oxygen, healing is accelerated.

Another benefit of **Exercise** is that wastes are more rapidly transported from the cells to organs of elimination via the bloodstream. The significance of this fact is that the blood pressure rises when wastes become stagnated in organs such as the kidney and liver.

The harmful results of stress have already been discussed under the section of Godly Trust. **Exercise** is one of the greatest remedies for stress. It relaxes the body, promotes sound sleep, and relieves tension and anxiety.

Without **Daily Exercise** the blood will become a stagnant pool of waste because of the lack of adequate circulation. It would be like never changing the oil in your car. Proper circulation is absolutely essential to the reversal of hypertension. Not only does exercise increase blood circulation, it also increases circulation within the lymph channels. The lymph is full of white blood cells and carries away the broken down products of fat metabolism.

Another benefit of exercise is that it is a key element in God's plan for obesity. Excess weight increases the pressure against artery walls because of the greater distance with which the heart must pump blood.

Walking is the best exercise because it brings all of our organs into use. A person should begin a walking program right away. Walk as far as is comfortable, and gradually work up to five miles a day. **Don't overdo it!**

A safe rule for walking is that you should barely be able to carry on a conversation with someone while you are walking. Another safety measure is that **if you develop chest pain during exercise, stop at that point.**

Exercise that benefits the heart and lungs is very important. The pulse should be raised to a safe level and kept there for twenty minutes by continuing the exercise. **To determine your safe pulse rate per minute, subtract your age from two hundred.**

Another very beneficial form of **Exercise** is **useful outdoor labor.** When God created mankind, He gave them useful labor as their exercise (See Gen. 2:15). All should learn the benefits of gardening and practice cultivating the soil. You will find that the angels will work with you, and you will experience an indescribable joy.

A rebounder has been found to be a very beneficial exercise too. Three to five minutes on a rebounder is the equivalent of one mile of jogging, and this exercise affects every muscle of the body. The good thing about rebounding is that your joints are not shocked with a sudden impact that would occur if you were running or jumping on a hard surface. When using a rebounder, be creative and try exercising different joints of the body while jumping.

In cases where a person is not able to perform any of the exercises listed above, massage is very beneficial. All forms of massage are passive exercises which increase circulation and relieve stress.

"Let us hear the conclusion of the whole matter!"
Ecclesiastes 12:13.

Daily exercise increases circulation which will supply the cells in the heart and blood vessels with their five needs (See page 16). Exercise is also an excellent remedy for stress which constricts blood vessels, increases heart rate and causes an increase in blood fats. Thirdly, exercise helps an obese person to lose weight, greatly reducing the distance which the heart must pump blood.

Sunshine

"But unto them that fear my name shall the sun of righteousness arise with healing in His wings."   Malachi 4:2.

God has placed remarkable healing power in Sunlight. **Sunlight** increases circulation, and also the volume of oxygen in the blood. The result is that the red blood cells carry more oxygen to the cardiovascular system and remove more toxins. This creates an internal environment which is very favorable to lowering blood pressure, providing energy and removing toxins.

Sunlight also increases the number of white blood cells in the body. Therefore, sunlight builds the immune system by sending more soldiers to fight on the battle field.

Sunlight also stimulates the liver which is a chemical laboratory able to detoxify poisonous substances from the body. Many of the toxins which the liver breaks down would clog this delicate organ if it was not stimulated by the sun.

Sunlight changes cholesterol to vitamin D, which is essential for the absorption of calcium in the body. As this cholesterol in the arteries is converted to vitamin D, the clogged arteries begin to open up.

Is there any wonder why the Bible says that, *"Unto them that fear my name shall the SUN of righteousness arise with healing in his wings." Malachi 4:2.*

Start with 10 -15 minutes a day exposing the face and hands to the sun. Gradually increase your exposure time to 30 or 45 minutes daily. DO NOT GET A SUNBURN! The best times for sunbathing are between 9:00 and 9:30 A.M. and between 4:30 and 5:30 P.M.

To avoid the risk of skin cancer, reduce the free fat intake, such as oils, margarines and other foods of this nature. It would be best to avoid these foods altogether.

"Let us hear the conclusion of the whole matter!"
Ecclesiastes 12:13.

Sunlight increases the oxygen content of the blood. Oxygen is necessary for repair, rebuilding and detoxification. Sunlight increases circulation and also increases the number of white blood cells. The life is in the blood. Sunlight stimulates liver function which detoxifies the body. A clogged liver increases hypertension in the portal vein which is reflected in the entire body.

Proper Rest

*"It is vain for you to rise up early, to sit up late, to eat the bread
of sorrows; for so He giveth His beloved sleep."*
Psalm 127:2.

Our bodies are composed of many trillions of cells. These cells group together to compose tissue. Tissues make up organs. Organs grouped together make up systems, and all the systems combined make the body. With this simple understanding, we can see that when the body is resting, the cells within the heart and blood vessels are also resting. In order for the cells to be healthy they must receive rest. It is during periods of rest that the tissues in the body are rebuilt and wastes are moved to points where they will be eliminated from the body. The walls of the blood vessels are made up of epithelial tissue and need rebuilding and repair to minimize the formation of atherosclerosis.

Without **Proper Rest,** energy will be used up by the cardiovascular system faster than it can be restored, tissue will be broken down faster than they can be rebuilt and poisons will be formed faster than they can be eliminated.

Ladies and gentlemen, do not these facts reveal that **Proper Rest** is essential to lowering blood pressure? *I REST my case!!!*

To help in the healing process, the digestive system especially is in need of rest. This can be accomplished by short periods of fasting with water, fruit and vegetable juices, herbs and raw foods. Because harmful dietary habits are the primary cause of hypertension, fasting on liquids is probably the fastest way to obtain results in a therapeutic program for high blood pressure. The twenty one day program mentioned later provides a nutrition schedule that has brought relief to thousands.

As far as sleeping is concerned, one hour of sleep before midnight is worth more for health's sake than two hours of sleep after midnight. We should retire before 9:30 to receive the best benefits from rest.

A relaxing soak in warm water will help you to relax if you have trouble getting to sleep. We should **avoid stress, confusion, television, and noise.** Also, if supper is eaten at all, it should be very light, (fruit and zwieback bread).

There is a relaxing herbal tea that one can drink without any sweetener just before going to bed . The formula for this tea is given below:

"Let us hear the conclusion of the whole matter!"
Ecclesiastes 12:13.

During periods of rest, the body repairs and rebuilds. Therefore, without **Proper Rest,** energy will be used up by the cardiovascular system faster than it can be restored, tissue will be broken down faster than it can be rebuilt and poisons will be formed faster than they can be eliminated.

Relaxing Tea Formula

1 Part Valerian
1 Part Scullcap
1 Part Hops
1 Part Vervain
½ Part Camomile
½ Part Peppermint

Mix herbs together. Boil water. Remove water from heat. Add 1 teaspoon of herb per 1 cup of boiled water. Steep for 10 minutes. Strain and drink tea.

Lots of Water

"If thou knewest the gift of God, and who it is that saith to thee, Give me to drink, thou wouldest have asked of Him and He would give thee living water." John 4:10.

To show the importance of water in providing answers to the arthritis dilemma, one need only ask, "What am I made of? The answer to this basic question reveals startling evidence in favor of consuming **Lots of Water.**

The body is seventy-five percent water. The vital organs are at least seventy percent water. The human brain and blood is eighty percent water. Other body fluids such as digestive juices, perspiration and urine are ninety percent water.

Water is needed to flush out sodium and wastes from the body via the kidneys and other organs. If we do not drink enough water, the body retains water in order to help eliminate the sodium and wastes. As this fluid is retained in the system, it increases the blood volume and causes the heart to have to pump more blood throughout the body. You might think of this as "watered down blood."

The Bible says that, *"The life of the flesh is in the blood." Leviticus 17:11.* Water taken internally increases circulation by thinning the blood. It also increases oxygen and blood volume. The more perfect the circulation, the more wastes are discharged from the body through the kidneys, skin and lungs. Water is also effective in reversing constipation, (a common problem accompanying almost all hypertension victims). Water is essential for normal bowel function.

Water can also be used externally to relieve the symptoms associated with high blood pressure. This is because water has the ability to cleanse the cells, eliminate wastes, and reduce stress.. Various parts of the body react in different ways to changes in water temperature. This point is graphically experienced when a person takes a warm shower, then alternates to a cold shower.

Obviously, bathing daily keeps the skin clean, but there are more benefits which can be derived from simple water treatments. Soaking in warm water causes constricted blood vessels to dilate. This therapy is also good for a heart that may be pumping too fast.

Jesus said, "I am Alpha and Omega, the beginning and the end. I will give unto him that is athirst of the fountain of the **water** of life freely." *Revelation 21:6*.

The application of water will be given in two sections. First of all, the internal use of water will be discussed. Secondly, we will discuss water and its external application.

The internal use of water

What kind of water should we drink? The answer to this question is **"Distilled water is the best water to drink."** The rain water that God has provided for us is actually distilled water. As water from the ocean evaporates and forms the clouds, this water actually has undergone a process of distillation. The reason why it is not recommended that people with hypertension drink rain water is that man has so polluted the atmosphere that as the water returns to the earth in various forms of precipitation, it is no longer in a pure state. Distilled water then is the water of choice. It absorbs many of the toxic substances and inorganic material and takes them out of the body.

Chlorine and Fluoride are poisons.

Drink Distilled Water

One should especially try to avoid water that has been treated with chlorine and/or fluoride. When sold over the counter, these chemicals carry the universal poison sign on the bottles. They suppress the immune system and should be avoided if possible. If it is not possible to obtain any other water, even water with chlorine and fluoride is better than no water at all.

Upon rising, drink two glasses of pure distilled water at room temperature with half a lemon in each glass.   During the day, one should drink water between meals being careful not to drink too close to mealtime. From one hour before each meal to two hours after each meal, we should not drink any water. This is because we don't want the water to interfere with the digestive fluids. **Do not drink water too hot or too cold.** If the temperature of the water is too extreme, the body will have to adjust the temperature of the water in the stomach before the body can use it. This taxes the nervous system and drains the body of necessary vital force.

The next step is to determine how much water we need to drink everyday. There is a very simple formula that a person can follow to determine the daily water consumption. **The formula is stated as your weight divided by two equals the number of ounces of water one should consume daily.** You can then divide this number by eight to determine the number of eight ounce glasses of water one should drink everyday.

Therefore, if a person weighs one hundred and sixty pounds, he needs to drink eighty ounces of water a day. This would be ten 8 oz glasses of water. This formula is used to determine the minimum amount of water that a person needs. If people perspire a lot they should increase their water intake even beyond the normal amounts. If the urine is not pale,  this is often an indication that more water is needed by the body.

What many have found to be a helpful practice is to **carry water with them wherever they go.** If you are not at home during the day, keeping your water with you in a jug, a jar or another type of container can really be a lifesaver.

The external use of water

Take a warm bath for about twenty minutes. This lowers the blood pressure by dilating the blood vessels, lowering the heart rate and reducing stress.

**a relaxing soak in
warm water
lowers blood pressure**

"Let us hear the conclusion of the whole matter."
Ecclesiastes 12:13.

The body is 70% water. When the body lacks water, it will retain fluids in an effort to remove excess sodium and wastes from the body. Water increases circulation, cleanses the body and helps eliminate toxins. Water increases the oxygen content of the blood. Used externally, water increases circulation and dilates blood vessels.

Always Temperate

"And every man that striveth for the mastery is temperate in all things." 1 Corinthians 9:25.

The law of temperance is two fold. First it involves abstaining from all harmful substances. Secondly, it calls upon us to do in moderation the things that are good.

All harmful substances such as alcohol, tobacco, caffeine, etc., contribute to high blood pressure and should be eliminated. Alcohol destroys the liver, and the blood pressure rises when the liver function is hampered. All poisonous substances such as tobacco, caffeine, and even some medicinal drugs burden the liver which has the awesome responsibility of detoxifying these substances. Cigarette smoke also depletes the body of vitamin C which is essential to proper adrenal function. It has already been mentioned that the adrenals play a major role in the stress response and in the production of essential digestive juices in the stomach. (See Godly Trust for an explanation of how the adrenals affect blood pressure).

In addition to potential liver and kidney damage, the social drugs listed in the above paragraph increase the blood pressure by increasing the heart rate and constricting the blood vessels. God never intended for human beings to poison themselves with alcohol, tobacco, caffeine and other legal or illegal social drugs.

White sugar should also be eliminated from the diet because it depletes the body of B vitamins which is necessary for a healthy nervous system. The nervous system is directly involved with helping a person cope with stress. Also, as refined white sugar is ingested, it dramatically raises the blood sugar. This concentrated sugar is generally more than the body needs for its present energy requirements, and it is converted to fat which is stored in the body. This contributes both to obesity and to an increase in blood fats. Obesity raises blood pressure by adding miles of blood vessels through which the heart must pump blood. It takes more pressure to pump blood to the greater distances.

Refined white sugar also causes the body to overreact by secreting an abundance of insulin. The result is that the blood
sugar drops and the individual experiences the fatigue and "all gone" feeling associated with hypoglycemia (low blood sugar). To bring the blood sugar levels back up, the adrenal glands become over stressed as they send forth adrenalin which converts stored sugar in the form of glycogen back to usable blood sugar (glucose) in the liver and muscles. White sugar causes a type of drug induced stress which raises the blood pressure as does alcohol, tobacco, and caffeine.

Even things which are good should be done in moderation. Eating is good, but overeating causes food to become poison because the body can only handle so much. Overeating also causes obesity, and its relationship with high blood pressure has already been mentioned.   Studying positive subjects is good, but even the Bible informs us that, *"Much study is a weariness of the flesh." Ecclesiastes 12:12.*

A good motto for temperance would be, "ALL GOOD THINGS IN MODERATION."

The law of temperance is applied in two ways. **First of all, harmful habits must be eliminated. Secondly, we must learn to be moderate and balanced in all things that we do.**

Temperance is a broad principle which is discussed throughout this book. Whenever a harmful practice or substance is revealed, the law of temperance is being taught. Whenever moderation in a habit or practice is taught, this is also a principle of temperance. Whether it involves eating, drinking, sleeping, sunbathing, exercise or any other health issue, we are taught to be temperate in all things.

This section will discuss some of the points which are often overlooked but have a direct bearing on our spiritual and physical health. One area that people often overlook is that of dress. Popular fashion often dictates many health destroying habits which violate the law of temperance. A contributing factor to high blood pressure is a lack of circulation in the extremities. One of the contributing factors to this circulation problem is the wearing of clothing which leaves the legs and arms exposed to the weather. The imbalance of circulation causes the blood vessels in the legs and arms to constrict because these areas are generally cooler. This condition cause the blood to be pumped into the trunk area because it will be warmer than the extremities. This causes an imbalance of blood flow in the body resulting in congestion in the liver and kidneys and restricted blood flow to the extremities.

Remember, everything that is harmful should be avoided, including unhealthful food and drink, alcohol, tobacco, other drugs, etc.

To keep us in health, God designed that the law of temperance should also balance our sexual activity with our spouse. A contributing factor to hypertension in men is an overstimulation of the sexual/reproductive organs. With every ejaculation, there is a considerable amount of zinc which is lost. This mineral is required in order for the body to maintain the proper concentration of vitamin E in the blood. Vitamin E lowers blood pressure and is an overall help to the cardiovascular system.

For women, temperance in this area is a better alternative than oral contraceptives. Taking the birth control pill raises your blood pressure!

That which is good should be done in moderation. Never overdo anything! All good things in moderation is the law of heaven.

"Let us hear the conclusion of the whole matter."
Ecclesiastes 12:13.

Drugs such as caffeine, nicotine, and alcohol, increase the heart rate and constrict the blood vessels. Refined white sugar increases stress, blood fats and obesity. Overeating causes obesity. Exposing the extremities constricts the blood vessels in the legs and arms and causes the blood to stagnate in the liver and kidneys. Intemperance in sexual relations causes a loss of zinc in males. This mineral is necessary to help maintain proper concentrations of vitamin E. Vitamin E lowers blood pressure and benefits the cardiovascular system. For women, the birth control pill raises the blood pressure.

Nutrition

"Blessed art thou oh land when thy... princes eat in due season for strength and not for drunkenness." Ecclesiastes 10:17.

 Proper nutrition can be secured by eating foods from the original four food groups given in the Bible. God said, "Behold I have given you every herb bearing seed which is upon the face of all the earth, and every tree in the which is the fruit of a tree yielding seed; to you it shall be for meat." *Genesis 1:29.* The Bible also declared in the third chapter of Genesis and verse three, "Thou shalt eat the herb of the field."

Fruits, nuts, grains and vegetables provide the body with all the essential nutrients that will help to build good blood and to eliminate the "seven pressure points" which lead to high blood pressure. This is the diet that man originally consumed, and in paradise when there will be no more killing of man or beast, and no food processing plants, mankind will once again resume a natural, plant based menu. So why not begin now preparing for heaven!

To help you remember the proper diet in contrast to the erroneous dietary traps that most Americans ignorantly or willfully fall into, we encourage you to think **"SAD"** to represent the "**S**tandard **A**merican **D**iet," and think **"GLAD"** to represent "**G**od's **L**ife **A**ctivating **D**iet." The **SAD** is high in fat, high in protein, low in fiber, and low in essential nutrients. As a delightful contrast, **GLAD** is low in fat, low in protein, high in fiber and high in essential nutrients. The original four food groups (fruits, nuts, grains, and vegetables) fit into the category of **"GLAD,"** and if we in this country are going to reverse the enormously high statistics which reveal how many Americans suffer from high blood pressure, **G**od's **L**ife **A**ctivating **D**iet is what we need.

Why does "GLAD" help to lower blood pressure? First of all, GLAD is low in fat. If our diet is high in fat, we increase our levels of blood fats which in turn increases our risks of plaque formation. These plaque formations cause the blood to have to pass through smaller spaces and therefore increase the overall blood pressure. An interesting note that all should remember is that the only source of cholesterol outside of that which is manufactured by the body comes in the form of animal products. There is absolutely no cholesterol in natural foods.

A high fat diet also burdens the liver which is responsible for the metabolism of this excess fat. A clogged liver will impede the flow of blood through the portal vein causing portal hypertension which is reflected throughout the body. A high fat diet also causes cells to clump together making it harder for the blood to pass through the narrow streams and tributaries of the circulatory system in order to reach the cells. When cells of the body do not receive an adequate supply of oxygen due to the traffic

jam, the heart must pump harder and faster in an effort to oxygenate the body. The end result is high blood pressure. Last but not least, a high fat diet contributes to a high fat person. Obesity adds miles of blood vessels through which the heart must pump blood. It will require more pressure to pump the blood through longer distances.

The second reason why GLAD lowers the blood pressure is that it is low in protein. Generally speaking, we eat too much protein. High protein foods include most animal products, along with some nuts and beans, gluten, tofu and other foods. In contrast with carbohydrates and fats, the body requires more energy and nutrients to metabolize protein. If we consume more protein than the body is able to safely metabolize or if digestion is hindered through bad eating habits, the excess or undigested protein becomes poison to the body. A high protein diet affects the blood pressure by causing the body to retain fluids. Fluids are retained in an effort to assist the body in moving the toxins to organs where they can be eliminated. This increases blood volume and blood pressure. The toxic wastes mentioned above also add to the rush hour traffic effect of an impure blood stream.

Excess protein also gives our liver and kidneys an unnecessary workout because the liver must help to metabolize the protein while the kidneys help to excrete excess protein and some of its by products such as uric acid and urea. We have already discussed renal and portal hypertension and how these conditions influence our blood pressure.

Protein from animal sources is injurious to the body because along with the protein, most meats will also contain more phosphorus than calcium. This upsets the bodies normal ratio of calcium to phosphorus. Because

God's Life-Activating Diet

Low In
Fat

Low In
Protein

THE GLAD DIET

High In
Fiber

High In
Nutrients

Standard American Diet

High In
Fat

High In
Protein

THE SAD DIET

Low In
Fiber

Low In
Nutrients

phosphorus and calcium tend to stay in balance with one another, calcium leaves the bones in an effort to balance the rush of phosphorus that we added to the bloodstream. As this calcium moves through the blood vessels, some of it becomes trapped in the cholesterol and calcium plaques which cause hardening of the arteries and raises the blood pressure. It is also a known fact that calcium deficiency is linked to high blood pressure.

Excess protein also contributes to obesity. This is because the extra protein which the body cannot use is converted to fat in the body. This adds those miles of blood vessels and raises blood pressure as we have already mentioned previously. It is also important to note that the more protein is consumed, the more calcium is lost and a lack of this mineral increases blood pressure.

The last two aspects of the Standard American Diet which cause it to be a prescription for hypertension are that it is low in fiber and low in essential nutrients. A low fiber diet causes constipation which in turn places toxins into the bloodstream. These poisons also impede the progress of circulation. Low fiber foods are always low in essential nutrients. Such nutrients are necessary for healthy cardiovascular and nervous systems.

Whole grains which are lacking in the **(S.A.D.)** are a very good source of B vitamins. B vitamins are necessary for a healthy nervous system and adrenal glands. You might remember that the adrenals are necessary for a proper stress response. With a lack of nutrients, normal stress becomes distress and the complications of high blood pressure such as constricting blood vessels and increased heart rate intensify. Whole grains are also a good source of potassium along with apricots, dried fruits, and some vegetables. Potassium is necessary to help bring the sodium into balance. Without enough potassium in the body, fluids will be retained which will raise the blood sugar.

Green leafy vegetables are high in calcium which helps to lower blood

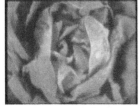

pressure. These vegetables should be eaten freely although not with a fruit meal of course.

One item that should be avoided is table salt along with processed foods containing sodium. This is because the salt increases blood volume and the impact of such an increase has been discussed in the seven pressure points.

The use of herbs also falls under the category of nutrition. The Bible says, *"He causeth the grass to grow for the cattle, and herb for the service of man." Psalm104:14.* Speaking of the tree of life, it was written that, *"The leaves of the tree were for the healing of the na-*

tions. " Revelation 22:2. Some herbs which the Creator has caused to grow for the service of those suffering from hypertension include hawthorn berries, cayenne, and garlic. M.E.E.T. Ministry provides an herbal formula containing the herbs listed above with a few other essential ingredients which you may obtain by contacting the office. The address and phone number are listed near the beginning of the book. M.E.E.T. Ministry also provides several natural foods cookbooks that will help you to change your eating habits by providing you with essential recipes to assist you in your transition. As you make changes in your eating habits, the following guidelines will help to direct your food choices.

1. **No refined foods:**
    No oil, margarine, shortening.
    No sugar, syrup, or free starch.
    No white bread, white rice, or degerminated corn meal.
    No store bought meat substitutes—gluten or soy types.

2. **No animal products:**

    No meat, fish or fowl.
    No eggs or egg yolk
    No milk products - milk, cheese, cream, ice cream, etc.

3. **Special items NOT allowed:**

    No alcoholic beverages, tea, coffee, or cola drinks.
    No sprayed, sulfured, or canned (in metal) fruit.
    No canned or frozen juices.
    No peanuts or peanut butter.
    No sprayed or canned vegetables. When fresh vegetables are
    not available, frozen are preferable to foods canned in tin or other
    metals.
    No night shades: (green peppers, eggplants, white potatoes).
    These foods may not affect every individual, therefore, you must
    experiment and see.

    **Note: All food should be fresh, unspoiled, "organically
    grown" as far as possible. The object is to avoid insecti
    cides and other sprays as well as to get produce with the
    best balance of trace minerals from the soil.**

4. **The allowed foods are:**

    All fruit, preferably fresh. Second choice are fruits canned in
    glass with fruit juice or water packed.
    All greens, especially cabbage, broccoli, turnip greens, mustard

greens, collard, or kale.

Use spinach, chard, or beet greens sparingly because of oxalate content.

All herbs that are mild.

All legumes (beans, peas, lentils, and garbanzos).

All whole grains. You need two kinds daily plus a legume to get optimal balance of amino acids.

Nuts in moderation. The better ones are the nontropical nuts such as almonds, filberts, pecans, and walnuts.

5. All nutritional needs on a PREVENTIVE type diet can be secured from daily servings of the foods listed below:

A citrus fruit plus another fruit.

A yellow vegetable such as carrots, etc.

A green vegetable, greens or herbs

A legume

Two types of whole grains

Tubers and nuts may be added as desired by the appetite

21 Day Nutritional Program

The fastest results from applying GOD'S PLAN to hypertension are generally experienced with a short termed liquid diet. This is a part of a 21 day nutritional program for high blood pressure. This nutritional program helps to lower harmful cholesterol levels, unclog arteries, decrease excessive blood volume and even lower stress. One can follow this program for three weeks, then refer to the "GOD'S PLAN Basic Menu" included in this booklet as a follow-up nutritional menu planner.

Days 1-2

For the first two days drink water and lemon water. Mix 6 oz of fresh squeezed lemons into 36 oz of distilled water. Your weight divided by 2 will give you the total amount of water that you need to drink daily. The lemon water may be substituted for some of the daily intake of water.

Day 3

Continue drinking water and lemon water, but one can add potassium broth at meal times if desired.

Day Four

Breakfast	2 servings of raw fruit. 1 serving of dry, whole grain bread.
Dinner	Raw fruit or vegetables 2 servings Bread 1 slice
Supper -	Optional: Potassium broth, fruit, or fruit salad. Zwieback can be eaten with this. (See God's Plan Basic Menu for zwieback recipe).

__Potassium Broth__ - Blend 1 cup of raw rolled oats with 3 cups of water. Strain the liquid and use as a base in which to cook the following vegetables chopped into large pieces: 1 white potato, 2 stalks of celery, 1/3-1 whole onion, 3 carrots, and a handful of parsley. Cook vegetables until carrots and potatoes are soft enough to be mashed. (It is not necessary to mash the vegetables.) Strain the liquid and drink the broth. It may be seasoned with

Braggs Liquid Aminos.

Day Five

<u>Breakfast</u>   Fruit meal (according to GOD'S PLAN Basic Menu)

<u>Dinner</u>   Vegetable meal (according to GOD'S PLAN Basic
              Menu)

<u>Supper</u>   Optional: Potassium broth, fruit, or fruit
              salad. Zwieback can be eaten with this.
              (See God's Plan Basic Menu for zwieback
              recipe).

Day Six through Twenty-One

Begin maintenance diet. Refer back to #5 for the recommended diet to
prevent high blood pressure. Refer also to GOD'S PLAN Basic Menu as
a guideline in your food preparation.

Special instructions:

Cook in stainless steel, Corning ware, or pyrex glass
No aluminum cookware
Avoid microwave
No pressure cooking
No "irradiated" produce

.General rules for good digestion are as follows: Eat slowly, chew your
food thoroughly, to allow the saliva to mix with the food. Avoid liquids
with meals. These decrease the flow of saliva with its digestive enzymes.

GOD'S PLAN Basic Menu

I. BREAKFAST:

Cooked Grain: - such as one of the following: Millet, Brown Rice, Barley, Rolled Oats, Buckwheat, Spelt, Quinoa.

Fresh Fruits: - Select 2-3 kinds - especially apples.

Fruit Sauce or Spread: - Mix 2 fruits in a blender-for sweetener add raisins or dates - (If a person has diabetes or hypoglycemia, do not eat dried fruits - omit).

Almonds: - 8-10

Seeds: - Sunflower, pumpkin, or sesame seeds. 1 Tablespoon.

Optional Grain or nut milk:

How to make grain milk

Grain milk: millet or brown rice
1 Cup of cooked grains
2-3 Cups of water (amount of water determines thickness)
(optional) - a pinch of salt for flavor
(optional) A little raw honey or a few dates for flavor
Blend until liquid.

How to make nut milk

1 Cup raw nuts or seeds
3-4 Cups of water (amount of water determines thickness)
(optional salt, honey and dates as given in grain milk recipe)
Blend until liquid.

II. LUNCH:

Cooked Grain: One of the following: Brown Rice, Corn, Millet or Potato (Baked or Boiled), or Whole Grain Pasta

Steamed Green vegetables: or cooked fresh peas or beans

Raw Salad: Leaf lettuce or Romaine - along with carrot sticks, celery, radish, green peppers, plenty of sprouts

Salad Dressing: Mix fresh lemon juice, honey, onion powder and garlic powder to taste. Add a little water to make it light.

How to make Sunflower Seed Dressing:

Whiz in blender until very creamy:

1 2/3 cup water	1 tsp. salt (optional)
1/2 tsp. garlic powder	1 tsp. onion powder
1 cup sunflower seeds	1/3 cup lemon juice, fresh is best.

Bread - Whole Grain - Optional

III. SUPPER:

Very light — Five hours before bedtime

Potassium broth, fruit or fruit salad with zwieback whole grain bread.

Zwieback means twice baked. Slices of bread are baked in the oven at a low temperature (150-200°) until crisp. This process changes the starch into a more easily digestible simple sugar.

"Let us hear the conclusion of the whole matter."
Ecclesiastes 12:13.

The Standard American Diet (SAD) has four categories of problems which are dangerous to a person with high blood pressure. First of all, the high fat increases blood fats. These fats clog arteries, lead to obesity, cause blood cells to clump together, and place a burden on the liver. No cholesterol can be found in natural foods.

Secondly, the ("S.A.D.") is high in protein. Excess protein is poison to the body and causes the body to retain more fluids in order to eliminate the wastes. A high protein diet places a burden on the liver and the kidneys. Because excess protein is stored as fat in the body, this diet contributes to obesity. Although not directly related to protein, the calcium to phosphorus balance is upset when a person consumes meats. The excess phosphorus causes calcium to leave the bones in an effort to balance the phosphorus. As this calcium travels through the blood vessels, it contributes to plaque formation.

The last two problems that the ("S.A.D.") causes the hypertensive person to face is that of low fiber and low essential nutrients. Without fiber we become constipated and without essential nutrients we cannot have a healthy cardiovascular or nervous system. Specific nutrients helpful for high blood pressure are found in fruits, nuts, grains, and vegetables. They include green leafy vegetables high in calcium (there is a link between calcium deficiency and high blood pressure), dried fruits and apricots high in potassium which helps to balance sodium, whole grains high in B vitamins and potassium, and herbs such as hawthorn berries, cayenne, and garlic.

Salt and high sodium foods should be avoided.

GOD'S PLAN DAILY PROGRAM
for HIGH BLOOD PRESSURE

6:00 AM   Devotion - Herbal tea or capsules from M.E.E.T.

7:00 AM   Leaves of Life Intestinal Cleanser
                 Mix in 1 tsp. Leaves of Life Herbal Cleanser to water
                 (Leaves of Life avail. thru M.E.E.T.)

7:30 AM   Breakfast - See basic menu plan included in this
                 booklet (For days 1-3 follow 21-day nutritional plan).
                 BEFORE BREAKFAST - 1 TBS Blackstrap
                 Molasses
                 AFTER BREAKFAST - Walk

9:00 AM   Sunlight - (15-20 minutes), then REST

10:00AM   Herbal tea or capsules from M.E.E.T.

12:00AM   Leaves of Life Intestinal Cleanser
                 Mix in 1 tsp. Leaves of Life Herbal Cleanser to the
                 tea (Leaves of Life avail. thru M.E.E.T.)

12:30PM   LUNCH - See basic menu plan included in this
                 booklet. (If fasting, drink water or juice)
                 BEFORE LUNCH - 1 TBS Lecithin, 1 TBS
                 Blackstrap Molasses

2:30 PM   Herbal tea or capsules from M.E.E.T.

5:00 PM   Walk - Sunlight

5:30 PM   Leaves of Life Intestinal Cleanser
                 Mix in 1 tsp. Leaves of Life Herbal Cleanser to the
                 tea (Leaves of Life avail. thru M.E.E.T.)

6:00 PM   Optional Supper - This will be either potassium
                 broth or fruit (Juices or water when fasting)

7:00 PM   Walk - Devotion

8:00 PM   Warm soak in the bathtub

9:00 PM   Bedtime

Power to Change

We _desire_ to do better. We know we **must** do better. We even **_try_** to do better. But all our efforts are as ropes of sand that break with the slightest resistance. We cannot seem to stop eating that ice cream that contains refined sugar. We cannot seem to resist that sirloin steak high in fats and cholesterol.

Multitudes long for a better life, but they lack courage and resolution to break away from the power of habit. They shrink from the effort and struggle and sacrifice demanded, and their lives are wrecked and ruined. But there is hope.

THERE IS POWER TO CHANGE!!

First we must acknowledge that we cannot do it by ourselves. Despite our repeated failures, this is perhaps the hardest step. We all like to believe we can do it by ourselves, that we don't need any help. But we need a Power above and beyond ourselves in order to change our life-style and live a healthy, happy life. And that power is Christ Jesus.

When we realize we cannot do it ourselves, we can then go to Christ for help. He will supply the power because He has promised to do so in _Matthew 28:18_, "All power is given unto me in Heaven and in earth." Indeed, your very desire to change is proof that He is ready and willing and wanting and able to provide you with all the power to change, "For it is God which worketh in you both to will and to do of His good pleasure." (Philippians 2:13).

Next, we must trust God that He will do what He says. This is faith, and "without faith it is impossible to please Him: for He that cometh to God must believe that He is, and that He is a rewarder of them that diligently seek Him." (Hebrews 11:6).

As we trust Him, as we put our faith in Him and not in ourselves, we must then step out in faith and not violate His laws of health. Jesus gives us strength to do this only one day at a time - "...as thy days, so shall thy strength be." (Deuteronomy 33:25). Although all the power is His, the decision to avail ourselves of His power always remains with us. As the children of Israel before they entered the earthly Canaan, you must "Choose you this day whom ye will serve; whether the gods which your fathers served that were on the other side of the flood, or the gods of the Amorites, in whose land ye dwell [which included the "gods" of feasting, intemperance, and appetite]: but as for me and my house, we will serve the Lord." (Joshua 24:15). We must choose to serve the Lord if we are to enter the Heavenly Canaan.

A lesson from nature illustrates the power of our Creator God to effect change.

The caterpillar is probably not one of the world's most beautiful creatures, yet the caterpillar has the potential to be transformed into an exquisite butterfly. The actual term for the transformation of a caterpillar to a butterfly is the Greek word *metamorphosis*. Paul used this same Greek word which we translate as transformed in *Romans 12:2*: "...be transformed by the renewing of your mind, that you may prove what is that good and acceptable and perfect will of God."

This transformation starts with an action of the mind, a conscious decision. Everything depends on godly thoughts and thinking patterns because they have the ability to transform our habits and actions according to God's Plan "for as he thinketh in his heart, so is he." (Proverbs 23:7).

 We must make a searching and fearless inventory of our habits and life-style, admitting to God and ourselves the exact nature of our wrongs, humbly asking God to remove our shortcomings, being entirely ready for Him to work in us and for us.

Let's look at another important picture from nature that mirrors what happens when we work together with God in following His plan for our health and happiness. This picture is of something that happens in every cell in our body.

Imagine a typical cell in our body by thinking of a circle. Attached to the outside of this circle are a number of receptor points. Floating around near the cell are hormones and enzymes that have indentations that exactly fit the shape of the receptor points. When a hormone or enzyme grasps hold of a receptor point, it has a special ability to stimulate a cell's activity. This stimulation is called "positive cooperativety."

When we cooperate with God by receiving His power, our bodies and minds are stimulated to activity in following His health laws. When the temptation comes to eat or do anything that will violate the laws of God, we must pray and ask God for the power to resist. And then, knowing that He has heard and answered our petitions, we ***must*** walk away. We ***must*** push away that plate of dainties. We ***must*** honor God by removing ourselves from the temptation as far and as often as possible. Once we do this, it becomes easier for us to repeat this action.

Through prayer and meditation on God's Word, we improve our conscious contact with Him. Thus we are better able to understand His will for us and can avail ourselves of the power which He so freely offers us.

In all this, and through this, we will learn to love the Lord and love Him more. God has promised, "Whereby are given unto us exceeding great and precious promises: that ***by these ye might be partakers of the divine nature***,

having escaped the corruption that is in the world through lust (2 Peter 1:4, emphasis added)." And what is the divine nature but a nature of divine love, for "God is love." (see 1 John 4:18, 19).

Loving obedience to God's laws of health results in the restoration of a measure of health for a better life here and a preparation for eternal life with Him forever. Although all the power is God's, the decision to use it lies with us. The miracle is that God's Plan for our lives works. It may not be fully explained, but it can be fully experienced.

God has pledged Himself to keep this human machinery in healthful action if the human agent will obey His laws and cooperate with God.

As you cooperate with God, you will be convinced that:

G.O.D.'S. P.L.A.N. CAN REVERSE HIGH BLOOD PRESSURE, THE SILENT KILLER!

BIBLIOGRAPHY

Holy Bible - King James Version

Baker, Elizabeth, "The Unmedical Miracle - Oxygen," Elizabeth Baker; Drewood Publications, 1991

Balch, James, F., M.D., and Phyllis, A, CNC, "Prescription For Nutritional Healing," James F. Balch, M.D., Phyllis A. Balch, CNC; Avery Publishing Group, Inc., New York, 1990

Donsbach, Kurt W., Ph.D., D.Sc., N.D., D.C."Heart Disease," The International Institute of Natural Health Sciences, Inc. 1980, **Morton Walker, DPM,"Negative Ions,"** Wholistic Publications, Mexico 1991.,**"Oxygen,"** Rockland Publications, 1993.

Hoover, Jerry, N.D., "Natural Medicine," KNI Printers, CA. 1993.

Kyme, Zane, "Sunlight"

"Mayo Clinic Family Health Book," IVI Publishing, Inc., 1993

Mowrey, Daniel B., PhD., "The Scientific Validation of Herbal Medicine," Kadts Publishing Inc. CT. 1986

Myerson, Ralph, M., M.D., "How Your Heart Works," Ziff - Davis Press, CA. 1994

Robbins, John, "Diet For A New America," Stillpoint Publishing, NewHampshire, 1987

Tenney, Louise, M.H., "Today's Herbal Health, 3rd Edition,"** Woodland Books, UT 1992

The Cholesterol Facts, A Joint Statement By The American Heart Association and the National Heart, Lung and Blood Institute.

Thibodeau, Gary, A. and Parker, Catherine, A., "Structure and Function of the Body, Eighth Edition," Times Minor/Mosby College Publishing, MO. 1988

Trattler, Ross, N.D., D.O., "Better Health Through Natural Healing," Thorsens Publishing Group, England, 1985

White, E.G., "Ministry of Healing," Pacific Press Publishing Assoc., ID. 1942

White, J.G., "Abundant Health," Published by Author

Williams, Redford, M.D., Williams, Virginia, PH.D., "Anger Kills,"Harper Collins, Publishers, Inc. New York 1993

COME ASIDE AND REST AWHILE

M.E.E.T. Ministry has developed a home-like health center in the peaceful countryside of West Tennessee. We call the center *Our Home* Health Center. It provides a 18 day program designed specifically to meet the physical and spiritual needs of each guest. These needs may include systemic illnesses such as cancer, diabetes, hypertension, arthritis, obesity and lupus. Our staff is also experienced in counseling in areas of stress management, depression, substance abuse, as well as overcoming smoking.

Each day our guests are educated through instructional classes. They learn how to prepare nutritious and appetizing vegetarian meals. We instruct them in the concept of GOD'S PLAN, what it is and how to apply it to their everyday lives. Juice therapy, hydrotherapy, herbal therapy, massage, along with outdoor exercise in the garden are incorporated into each session.

Upon completion of the 18 day program, each guest not only begins to learn how to cooperate with God for physical restoration, but they also have found new family members whom they cherish.

If you or someone you know would like to come aside and rest awhile and take advantage of what we offer at *Our Home*, please contact us at least three weeks in advance of the starting date.

M.E.E.T. Ministry, 480 Neely Lane Huntingdon, TN 38344
(731) 986-3518, FAX (731) 986-0582.
E-mail: godsplan@meetministry.org
WebSite: www.meetministry.org

Would You Like to M.E.E.T.?

WHAT IS M.E.E.T. MINISTRY?
MISSIONARY EDUCATION AND EVANGELISTIC TRAINING

M.E.E.T. Ministry is a Christian health ministry. We believe from inspiration and research that most of our sickness is the result of our departure from G.O.D.'S. P.L.A.N. and that only in obedience to the laws of God, both natural and spiritual, can true health be restored or preserved. Our ministry conducts health seminars of varying duration, along with cooking schools and training workshops. Our focus is "training," and with God's help, we seek to prepare others to be health missionaries. Our training culminates with a four month training school held once a year on our country property in Tennessee. M.E.E.T. is a self-supporting ministry. Although we do accept donations, we seek to sustain our ministry with industries which provide income and bless the community as well.

We would love to MEET you! If you would like to schedule a seminar for your church, social group, etc., we would love to come and share how GOD'S PLAN affects, obesity, arthritis, drug addictions of all kinds, and every other ailment which is bringing suffering and death to millions everyday. So how do we MEET? Just contact our office for details. It's that simple!

M.E.E.T. Ministry, 480 Neely Lane, Huntingdon, TN 38344
(731) 986-3518, FAX (731) 986-0582.
E-mail: godsplan@meetministry.org
WebSite: www.meetministry.org

GOD'S PLAN – HEALTH AND HAPPINESS LIBRARY SERIES

* FROM S.A.D. TO G.L.A.D.
Natural Foods Cookbook

*God's Plan: The Answer to Cancer
*God's Plan for taking the "Itis" out of Arthritis
*God's Plan for High Blood Pressure, The Silent Killer
*God's Plan for Obesity, Winning The Battle Of The BULGE
*God's Plan Gives Freedom From Addictions
*God's Plan for Those Sugar Blues, Diabetes and Hypoglycemia
*God's Plan Overcomes Osteoporosis, No Bones About It!
*God's Plan for Arresting Allergies
*God's Plan for Parkinson's, When life gets a little shaky
*God's Plan for AIDS, There's H.E.L.P. for H.I.V.
*God's Plan for Alleviating Lupus
*God's Plan for Multiple Sclerosis
*God's Plan for Hormone Harmony, From Hot Flashes to Monthly Crashes
*God's Plan for Constipation, The Mother of All Diseases
*God's Plan for Conquering Candida

PLUS TAPES AND VIDEOS

<u>Note: This complete series is in the process of development.</u>
To be notified by mail every time a new booklet, video, or tape is completed,
please contact our office and ask to be placed on our mailing list.
(Our Address, Phone and Fax Numbers are listed in the front of this book).

Notes

Made in the USA
Las Vegas, NV
18 May 2022

49039722R00036